Scribbles & Sonnets

A Multitude of Selves

Danielle Larson

BookLeaf Publishing

India | USA | UK

Made with ❤ on the BookLeaf Publishing Platform
www.bookleafpub.in
www.bookleafpub.com

Dedication

To:
the password kids,
the unappreciated moms/wives/partners,
the regular kids,
the parentified kids,
the lonely kids,
the neurodivergent,
the girls, gays, and theys
those who feel the need to escape

I see you.

Preface

These poems are fingerprints left on fogged glass—
intimate markings of identity, desire, and disconnect.
They trace the outline of a self learning to exist in spaces
between masks, exploring the tension between public
performance and private truth.

Within these pages, you'll find verses that slip between
shadows and light, between certainty and doubt. They
chronicle a journey through the complexities of being
seen and unseen, of carrying weights that were never
meant to be carried, and of finding strength in
vulnerability.

Some pieces emerge from places of raw exposure—
confessions whispered in midnight hours, memories that
refuse to fade, and moments of fierce authenticity
breaking through carefully constructed facades. Others
dance with passion and power, celebrating the electric
current that runs beneath polite society's skin.

This collection doesn't offer neat resolutions or
comfortable conclusions. Instead, it invites you into the
beautiful mess of becoming—into spaces where identity

shapeshifts, where desire burns bright enough to leave marks, and where healing sometimes means first acknowledging the wounds.

These are more than poems; they are artifacts of transformation, documenting the endless process of unmaking and remaking oneself in a world that often demands we be less than we are.

Welcome to the space between heartbeats.

Acknowledgements

My family for endless inspiration.

Also:

C.K. my favorite writing buddy, beta reader, and fellow transplant

S.D. my best and most cherished friend!

S.F. my internet bestie and meme sharer.

My coworker friends past and present whom always made the days bearable.

"Dream job? I simply do not dream of labor."

"We live on a rock floating through space, we should be doing cool sh*t instead of work."

1. The Artist

scribbles in margins
doodles drawn from restless hands
words and fragments escape mental confines
falling together in delicate patterns
a sonnet, etched in ink
constellations dotting skin
each splinter of wisdom
a new mark in memory preserved
living archive a temple
upon which moments collect
as sacred text
dancing across a blank canvas

2. I Am Not Cool

I am the millennial who never learned
how to be properly jaded—
still wearing skinny jeans like armor,
Doc Martens laced with defiance.

My playlists skip from Beatles to BTS,
Taylor Swift to Tool without apology;
I collect joy like others gather grudges,
wonder spilling from my overfull hands.

At forty, I'm all contradictions:
recovery and revelation,
daughter learning to mother herself
while mothering others.

My enthusiasm bursts in caps lock,
exclamation points pepper my texts
like confetti—I haven't learned
the art of being unimpressed.

I am high-rise pants and low-key anxiety,
Vans-wearing vocals singing in traffic,
finding myself in forgotten corners
between who I was and who I'm becoming.

Sister, lover, friend, and guide—
wearing multitudes like mismatched socks,
proud in my intentional chaos,
authentic in my uncertainty.

I am not cool—I am alive,
electric with the magic of existing,
refusing to dim my light
for those afraid of burning.

3. Mask

Their voices envelop me—
a borrowed coat, new skin,
seams stretched too tight across
borrowed bone;
threads of should-be tether what was,
while what-is slips through fingers like smoke

Speaking tones downloaded, practiced, stored:
[smile.exe] [laugh.exe] [care.exe]
Each gesture a line of code
compiled to render: human

Heat radiates from their living bodies
yet ice creeps through my manufactured panes
as echoes whisper: *you are not*
I am an outline, algorithm, air—
a shadow script compiled in flesh

Beneath this hollow, shifting space
I morph through infinite arrays of self
each mask a perfect forgery
while mirrors hold no truth to tell
just faces borrowed, voices staged
an echo chamber of the age

where authenticity dissolves.

I am the space between the words;
the static in the song—
the glitch inside the pattern
forever searching for my code
in others' reflections

Suspended in a chorus
alien in familiar skin
grasping for solidity
in a world where I do not fit in.

4. Matryoshka

Each hollow figure holds another—
grandmother's silence carved
from mirrors of self-obsession,
mother's words painted
in childish needs and absence,
my own shell decorated
with walls of steel independence

We nest inside each other's pain:
grandmother's wooden heart,
mother's porcelain masks,
my practiced words of self-reliance
Each generation a little smaller,
a little lighter, a little less burdened
by the weight of inherited wounds

I trace the lines of their faces,
seeing shadows of myself
in features worn smooth by time:
grandmother's hateful scowl
softening to mother's furrowed brow,
emerging as my cautious smile,
blooming in my daughter's occasional laugh

We are recovering matryoshkas,
each generation learning
to hold space for healing:
grandmother's entitled survival,
mother's stumbling growth,
my cynical repair

Understanding blooms
like hand-painted flowers:
their battles were not mine to fight,
their wounds were not mine to heal,
but their strength lives in my bones
as I break these ancient patterns
one layer at a time

5. The Inheritance of Care

My life was never my own to keep—
From maiden dawn to widow's night,
The weight of others makes me weep.

First came love's domestic sweep:
Children's needs, both dark and bright;
My life was never my own to keep.

One child's struggles cut so deep,
Special care my day and night,
The weight of others makes me weep.

Then aging family slowly creep
Into my home—"it's your duty, it's only right"
My life was never my own to keep.

My career dreams? They fell asleep
While husband's soared to greater height;
The weight of others makes me weep.

Now tending him as shadows steep,
Until my flame fades into night—
My life was never my own to keep,
The weight of others makes me weep.

6. Least Favorite

Third child, but first mistake
The one they stopped taking pictures of
While my sisters sparkled
I learned to disappear
Just lose some weight
Fix your hair
Stop being so sensitive
Why can't you be more like—

Childhood measured in comparisons:
Baby sister, the precious last
Middle sister, always laughing, forever funny
But first: me. Just me.

Too much and never enough
Three years in a darkness
Writing stories no one read
Sleeping away each day
Because being unconscious hurt less
Than being awake and unwanted

Church members at Christmas:
Oh, I didn't know you had three
As if I never existed

You chose to not be involved

Depression wasn't real
Just attention-seeking
Just being dramatic
Just needed to get over it
Just just just

School to home to bed
Repeat until numb
While they lived their lives
Around the hollow space
Where a daughter should have been

7. ATLAS

Offers of help are papercuts on thin skin—
sharp reminders of empty spaces
where support should have lived
I flinch from a words of praise
foreign to the judgemental mother tongue

I scatter assistance like seeds,
desperate to grow the wildflowers
I never got to tend;
watching others bloom
under the acceptance I never knew

But when your needs press against my walls,
something feral wakes inside me—
that child who held up her own sky
screaming: *I cannot carry another world*
when I am still learning to put mine down

Defined by productivity, by worth to others
the steady and wholly needed, unappreciated
the foundation stone who fears
the weight of being needed

Watch how I build castles for others

while sleeping in my ruins,
how I give away maps
while staying lost,
how I bleed myself dry
trying to fill cups that were
never mine to pour

8. Tempest

You're impossible, wild, a storm to control,
words slice flesh to soul
You argue, you rage, you refuse to obey—
One day you'll birth your own chaos, and then you will
pay

Venom drips daily, corroding my core,
dissolving what came before.
You're feral, ungrateful, a constant disgrace—
I don't know what I did, you never learn your place

Fold inward, crack and bend,
Origami daughter, too broken to mend.
Practiced indifference, hiding my care:
Be smaller, be silent, try not to be there

Rebellion still burned, fire in my blood,
Years of submission, becoming a flood.
Fled in the night, demons in tow,
Hopeful distance could dissolve what hatred did sow

Fate placed a daughter, wild-eyed in my arms,
A mirror reflecting forgotten alarms—
She blazed, a comet, untamed and aware,

Questions like daggers and lightning-struck hair

When she rages, I taste mother's words
Rising like bile, old lessons stirred.
Hands shake, echoes what was taught:
Break her, tame her, tie her in knots.

She dances, her own wild storm
Force of nature, the tempest formed
I see the truth of me destroyed:
A girl once as bright, a star in the void.

Cradled my wild one, thunder rolling deep,
Kiss lightning-crowned temples, finally she sleeps.
My fierce one, my brave one, I whisper at night,
Your fire's not wrong—it was always just right.

Tantrums and triumphs rewrite what I knew,
Old poisons dissolve in the dew.
My daughter's defiance—a gift set me free:
The child I was fighting was really just me.

Through her, discovered pieces once lost,
Spirit once frozen under mother's frost.
Watch her soar, unafraid, a siren song
My shattered self built her strong.

9. Cool

I am incapable of nonchalance—
my midnight texts burst with exclamation points,
each response an eager sunrise.

I swallow bitter almosts,
savor sugared maybes,
dancing on the knife-edge of your comfort zone,
flirting with disaster

I am a bleeding technicolor heartbeat
trapped in millennial gray,
too bright, too loud, too much—
an aurora in your muted sky.

Your safe harbor cannot hold me;
you wade into the storm,
tasting danger on your tongue
while I spin wild and electric—
I am a hurricane.

10. Too Much

I don't know how to love
with slow discovery and moderation—
these measured sips of knowing.

I only know consumption:
wanting to memorize every atom of your being,
to study the universes you contain,
to map the constellations of your thoughts.

I am unsuited for temperance—
I want to swallow stars,
to burn in understanding,
to achieve enlightenment
through the authenticity of your soul.

11. Professional

I laugh - smile on cue
Prompt, polite. Eyes almost glazed
Muse cries, this pays bills

12. The Hand Necklace

Encircling, a warm soft chain
Fingers curl their sweet dark reign
Pressing in, my breath grows week
Release as kisses claim my cheek

Grip, and every pulse obeys
Husky whispers through shadowed haze
A collar forged of flesh and bone
Claiming me as yours alone

Squeeze – a tethered, sacred thrill
Dance in power, time stands still
Velvet pressure, darkened gaze
Biting lips through pleasure's haze

Bruises bloom like midnight art
Vows emblazoned on my heart
Shape me, mold me, mark your claim
Into surrender's sweetest flame

No jewels could match this hungry hold
Your steady hands worth more than gold
This precious weight, this perfect bind
The anchor for my racing mind

13. In The Dark

Daylight movements, graceful ease
Visual poise, eager to please
Soft smiles, a voice so kind
Full of charm, sharp of mind

Measured steps, words precise
Apparent elegance, calm and nice
Subtle class in public gaze
Dancing through the daily maze

Behind closed doors where shadows play
A deeper chord claims its stage
Shedding every sweet veneer
Passion rising, strong and fierce

Silk and lace against hot skin
Sacred secrets burn within
Craving rhythm, yours with mine
As limbs and whispers intertwine

No harsh commands or cruel extremes
Just whispered demands and shared dreams
Grips both firm and gentle thread
Through darkness where desires tread

Two worlds, each pure, complete
Balance found through tart and sweet
Inner depths desires unfold
Into flames both soft and bold

14. Tidal

I held love in my arms,
a fragile weight against my chest,
heartbeat soft and steady,
the whisper of dawn.

I tasted joy,
sweet and sudden,
laughter spilling over the edges
of days too full to hold.

I know heartbreak,
the quiet shattering
their anguished cries,
voice I couldn't soothe,
a distance I couldn't cross

Frustration, a storm,
when defiance meets demand,
voices clash with mine,
sharp-edged and unrelenting
Boundaries being tested.

Give and give
until threadbare,

Patience worn thin
by the weight of endless demands.

Dancing in happiness,
spinning wild in sunlit rooms,
where tiny hands reach for mine,
the world endless,
each step a melody,
each breath a promise.

Sadness cuts deeper
their pain now my own,
their tears bruise
my heart,
I watch them struggle
and know I cannot shield them
from the world's sharp edges.

Lost in the weeds,
buried beneath to-dos,
sleepless nights,
pieces of me scattered
in the wake of their needs.

Who was I before?
Who am I now,
beyond mother? Beyond caregiver?

the architect of their world?

Mothering - a tide
Swelling, receding
Drowning, delivering
Carving weight into aging bones
Leaving me breathless
on the shore.

15. Exodus

Small town shadows stretch like prison bars
across bedroom walls that never felt mine—
a temporary shelter, not a nest,
where I perched like a bird about to flee

No tearful goodbyes or promises,
just a midnight departure on a train heading east
leaving nothing behind but
the shed skin of a teenage rebellion

They say roots anchor, but mine
were seeds waiting for wind—
scattered toward concrete canyons
where buildings glow brighter than the stars.

Years of chasing neon dreams
through metropolitan mazes
taught me: escape isn't in leaving,
but the freedom to choose your own chains

Now in my own quiet corner,
where city fades to forest edge,
I recognize these small-town rhythms—
not as chains, but as choice

Here, where trees provide shelter in my hillside
and neighbors wave but don't intrude,
I sow my dreams in fertile soil
that I alone have chosen.

Finally understanding:
home isn't where you're from
or even where you land—
it's who you've grown to be

16. January

Cotton candy skies unravel slow,
spun sugar bleeding soft on snow.
The earth below, a hollow ache,
a breath held tight, a smile I fake.

These fields remember what I've left—
my spirit raw, my heart bereft.
My shadow bends in salted air,
a ghost of girlhood trapped in prayer.

Beneath the weight of endless frost,
I wear my roles, their heavy cost.
Mother, daughter, sister, wife—
essential embroidery, seams of life.

The sky ignites, pink and blue,
tender things that I once knew—
the hunger, raw, beneath my skin,
the want, the ache, to start again.

The wind, it hums a hollow tune,
a lullaby, winter's croon.
And still, I trace the fading light,
a woman hidden in plain sight.

The snow, it swallows every sound,
secrets buried, never found.
And yet, the sky still dares to bloom,
a blush against the biting gloom.

I drive on through bitter cold,
through stories looped and love grown old,
but somewhere in the painted air,
a ghost of a girl, no longer there.

17. How To Be Extremely Normal Online

fact-checking your spotify wrapped
because 47,382 minutes seems low
(you've done the math three times)

chronically adding emojis and exclamations
so everyone knows you're cool and fun and friendly!

getting into niche drama
in a server about
a band that broke up in 2013
(you've memorized the entire wiki)

diagnosed with main character syndrome
but plotting to become the villain
because the aesthetic is better
and you're committed to the arc

3am and my brain be like:
[intrusive thought detected]
[opening 47 chrome tabs]
[falling down wikipedia rabbit hole]
[becoming an expert on medieval farming]
[organizing entire music library]

[by vibes AND alphabetically]
[simultaneously]

leaving "Me AF"
on posts about declining mental health
or send a post to a friend saying,
"Literally Us" about some unhinged behavior
while my screen time report
is basically a cry for help

still using tumblr in 2025
because you're either elite
or unable to let go
(it's definitely both)

Parsing life through forward slashes,
emotions tagged with perfect form—
/genuine //lighthearted /joking
/this-is-how-i-cope-with-the-dystopia-hellscape-we-live-
in

Watch me spiral through the vibes
(unhinged)
(feral)
(straight up not okay)
(living my best life bestie)
(ascending to a higher plane)

while I use TikTok to try to diagnose
my extremely abnormal brain

/hj but make it ❖ sparkly ❖ /srs

18. Thief!

I witness works that steal my breath—
masterpieces now measuring rods,
compositions of perfection that shatter
my reflection into shards of failure.

Their brilliance burns my retinas,
leaves afterimages in my dreams of everything
I'll never touch,
hidden under shadows, *better than*

My fingers shake above backlit keys,
brushes tremble in hesitant hands
as their genius reverberates in my skull,
drowning out my timid voice

Yet through these halls of greatness
the thief strips away,
each moment of pride, small victories,
inadequacies cloaked in bitterness

While I hide my heart's work
in folders marked "WIP,"
watching my own light flicker
in confidences' vacuum.

What bitter mathematics:
where esteem is paralyzed
by steady drops of "could be better"
until creation becomes punishment

Still I persist in quiet corners,
while my work remains hostage to
the relentless thief
who keeps my work for herself.

19. Perfection

You are everything
I am nothing but mistakes
Tell me how I'm wrong

20. Here's a Haiku!

You are just a man.
Basic, white, and generic.
Yet I dance for you.

21. I Would Simply Die

Here Lies Danielle
1984 - 2024

"I would simply die"
Narrator: She did

Living her best death
No thoughts, just vibes (eternal ones)
Main character energy (deceased)

Plot twist bestie:
Death wasn't just being dramatic